Inwood Winds

Poems from Upstate Manhattan

by

Steph Shearier

Grosvenor House
Publishing Limited

The right of Steph Shearier to be identified as the author of this
work has been asserted in accordance with Section 78
of the Copyright, Designs and Patents Act 1988

The book cover picture is copyright to Steph Shearier

This book is published by
Grosvenor House Publishing Ltd
Link House
140 The Broadway, Tolworth, Surrey, KT6 7HT.
www.grosvenorhousepublishing.co.uk

A CIP record for this book
is available from the British Library

ISBN 978-1-83975-339-8

For Magpie

TABLE OF CONTENTS

1. INWOOD WINDS

On wild nights
wind borne
notions are blustered into images
with each gust.

Strong streams steady from the North
scream over Van Cortlandt.
Inwood Hill's filtering wileful continental air.

Riverside buffets the
tidal torrents from Father Hudson.
Isham tonight stands imposing in black.
The GW Bridge is a taut high-strung glittery white
    diadem
against a sapphire sky
whence come breezes choppy, brazen.

The Eastern horizon is almost always
a stark line
when it is not a steel dark wall down to the ground.

Whistling they conspire to inspire.
Spirit is within
Inwood winds.

2. APPROACHING NOR'EASTER

It's on its way.
Long slung cold thrusts
slug you under the chin.

Slush snow smacks
nostrils and cheeks.

The gust wind from the North
slaps chips of frozen mist
to your mug
forcing your form
into the wind's essence.

3. SNOW STORM 27 JANUARY, 2004

Ridge in the Bronx
is abruptly
obliterated
with its every light.

All is quiet...
but for the occasional clanking and scraping of engines
and beeping.

Sheaths of snow
are swept
in patterns
across the horizon
shaped silent as the steady wind.

Imperious Boreas,
Mother Nature,
is soft.

She is generous in showing each snow flake
as a prism surprising
in all its hues...

through which
every light elicits
each color...

Thank her!

4. DAWN (haiku)

With the light the moon
seemingly without wanting
winked her eye good-bye.

5. SNOWFLAKE (haiku)

What say stray snowflake?
Your presents are too hasty.
You'll fade fast away.

6. FATHER WISCONSIN (haiku)

Father Wisconsin
swirls so wildly on his way,
frowns, then sleeps, then grins.

7. PEACE (haiku)

Peace is still the part
into the puzzle fit will
fill the whole with peace.

8. GINKGO TREE FOR MAGGIE (haiku)

Maggie, do you see?
Do you see our ginkgo tree
strong like you and me?

9. ZEN SMILE (haiku)

A brook wends its way.
The winds humor a whistle,
While wander ripples.

10. FELIZ NAVIDAD (haiku)

Estamos en mi casa
Feliz navidad!
bebiendo ron.

11. TO THRILL A MOCKINGBIRD

To thrill a mockingbird
you'd have to rondo like a robin,
stagger-tweet like a starling,
wheeze roundly like a warbler.

You'd have to croon like Nat King Cole, hog-holler like
  Minnie Pearl,
"Beep! Beep! Beep!" like a backing truck and "zisch!"
  and
"huusch" like escaping steam.

You'd have to be Bobby McFerrin
(lugubriously rising): "Djeep!"
"Tscheer! Tscheer!"
(whistle like a robin)
"Eenh, eeenh, eeenh".

To thrill a mockingbird
you'd have to be the most seasoned naturalist,
a supreme forager, the ultimate urban trapper.

You'd have to strut in a perfectly
tailored tux of the finest fabric,
sleek, muscular and handsome;
to flirt, tease and seduce;

a real killer,
a heart-breaker.

To thrill a mockingbird
you'd have to bob and weave like Smokin' Joe Frazier
up and down, back and forth, side to side.

You'd have to swoop and flit and twitch
lighter than an air thermal,
flashing like a snowflake,
glittering vertically, horizontally
more blithely than Tinker Bell.

You'd have to be gaudy, shiny, brilliantly-hued…
then the mockingbird would snatch you,
hide you
and
fawn over you.

12. SHAD EPIC

The instant the latest night winds lose their chill
root clusters are seduced to uncoil.
Channel currents warm the flanks and fill
the gonads of the Sea's Knights.

They roil with glee
from levee to levee.

The fight for light is now won.
Quickening dawns assume
the shad are on the run.
when the forsythias bloom.

In great balloons north along Father Hudson from
    the sea
agush with spawn
they're drawn,
so say the Lene Lenape.

Mother Earth's gifts swift,
brawny and smart,
new generations will start
like late winter's bonny child, the Zephyr.

Snag one, if you're clever,
cedar-roast it and use pepper.

Winter-weary souls are lusty
from warm, fragrant air.

"Paradise!" booming Spring declares.
"Now it must be..."

Time for shad the river's sacred squires,
who team all watery rooms,
while rosy-cheeked are dawns afire,
when forsythia blooms.

13. KATY-DID

"Katy did!
Katy didn't."

Through the hottest, heaviest, deepest Summer nights
ratcheting
up the scale
down the scale...
a chronometer!

In the larch down the hill in the park,

"Katy did!
Katy didn't!"

Answer from London Plane on the slope
just beyond the fieldstone wall:

"Katy did!"

Did we say we did?

"Katy didn't!"

Hidden
forbidden...
Did I tell her, "I didn't?"
Midst shadowy tree-lined silhouettes and twinkling
    specter of GW Bridge, when every whisper offers a

mystery, I'm like a turret spinning to listen to the startling questions, surprisingly loud, posed in an incremental upward/downward ratcheting as if on an ancient wooden cogwheel.

"Katy did?
Katy didn't?"

I'll give you secret ribbons for your ginger hair.

14. WARBLERS (March, 2002)

Are those the warblers
we hear
singing in the Spring?

Tschi, tschioo, tschwee
Tschi, tschiwoo, tschwee
[falling] de de dri di
[rising] dee dee dree di

Warblers occupy our woods
as always again
after every long, uncertain winter.

Now it is a dark hour.
This time is filled with sounds
driving deep into the ground.
[chorus] Boom! Booom! Bbbboooomm!

War blurs.

Claims to digital fame
and minimum loss of limbs
and that they
cannot display
the same
values as Uncle Sam
is to say they are so stupid
not to know an invasion
from a hot fudge sundae.

To tell lies
then wave red, white, blue,
they are as mockingbirds
flashing black against white.

War blurs.

The rumbling, pounding of bullying
heavy vehicles

[chorus] Boom! Booommm! Booom!
and various vainglorious
assertions of success
while senses are singed, skewed, sacrificed
still can never match the precision
in the perfect harmony
of amassed warblers

Tschii, tschii, tschich, tzwoo

taking over late at night
in the lull
at the time when all are asleep
when everyone's dreaming,
when noises don't disperse.

When all aberrations assert
still dishonest power,
warblers wizen the widening dawn,
winging in their beauty

Tschii, tschwiouh, tschwee!
Tschii, tschoo, weee, tschooo

and then
in a nod again
they are gone.

15. STARLINGS (for Maggie, Richard and Dennis)

Starlings switch and swirl in murmurations
settling suddenly twittering and chirping in myriad
    conversations
then swirl again
in undulating, twirling shifts,
rising in geodesic shapes,
then falling fast
in spiraling silhouettes
slowly spreading throughout the slate, grey sky...
on late cooling summer evenings.

As they gather in ever swarming numbers
lighting but briefly
touching the tops of the cottonwood trees
lining the river
silent a second...
they startlingly swoop in every which way
fixed unwaveringly in their eyes
flying fast wing to wing
the next other seven
starlings...
on cooling late summer evenings

16. DER OTTER

Linguaized francophilia
softens our familiarity with the otter,
who is odder and harder
than any other furry beast
you'll ever see around here.

Der Otter possesses
webbed feetesses...
like platypuses' zasses.

The otter is always more than one
most often two.
So it is the otter: they
roil wrestling round the other,

slip glide
down back slides
of the glitch mud ooze
all over the holds
of the Namakagee.

In full sunlight...
flecks crisp from mauve to sable
to martin brown in sharp cast
shard beads
glisten
sinewy muscled forearms
springing to bat snapping nostrils
of playmates.

Sleuths swimming
among algae
after fish
as fish
in the subterranean chiaroscuro
they are like seals.

Der Otter is never
within clear earshot.

On occasion one once
imagined a nattering,
natt-, nattering
while they gnashed
on their backs
floating cuddly-faced with
plenty of pointy hard, sharp teeth
breath of fish and frog
and cattail root husks on a mollusk.

At a distance usually
they will move mercury.

It is their patented beau geste.

17. PETE SEEGER: IN MEMORIAM

You don't know
  whether workers are stronger
  whether bosses are more thoughtful
  whether symbols succeed
  whether our melting pot is more mellow
  whether races smile as they strive side by side.

You don't know
  whether there is more justice
  whether women are more honest
  whether men are more true
  whether folks are more fair
  or whether there are fewer wars.

You do know
  that humility is powerful
  that trash-talk is no help
  that bravery is menacing
  that swagger is just silly
  and modesty is generous.

You know
  there is a lightness to your step
  a smile upon your face
  a hope-filled tune within your head
  that the Hudson flows more sweetly
  that significant sloops are in place
  and that dick-dock-dori
  all un-American

reaction
cannot daunt you,
that there is wisdom to the Weavers of the wild
and that sometimes even Don Quixote will win
and you outlast
the bastards.

18. THE ROBBERY OF CHARLIE CHAPLIN'S GRAVE (1978)

Somebody robbed Charlie Chaplin's grave,
dug him up and hauled him afar
to make one last film to public raves
with Charlie as the quiet star.

They tippy-toed under the cover of night
soundlessly through the graveyard at Vevey
and effortlessly took Charlie in flight
for at his age he wasn't heavy.

To be neither funny nor violent,
this last film with Charlie would only be silent.

Like Beckett's "Breath" but sans screams
a coffin cast on a naked studio set
would call all to register their reverent best
for Charlie's eternal pleasant dreams.

19. THE PRINCIPLE OF POONTANG

When you been groovin' too long
on the poon
you start thinkin' that
that tang thang
be lookin' kinda' good,
start lookin' like
DAMN!

That thang makes you
always wanna live
under
below and
away from that
drive to survive,

only
starts makin' you look at that
tang.
The tang thang that cools you,
that poontang
that holds you close
may be the only thang that
after the seething rage
can smooth you
soothe you
make you ooze.

20. DAS SAY A DONK (a sound poem)

Das say a Donk
Wo nay a Konk
No sana Doo
A seigh way.

Plees sed a flork
Yu kaem her glork

O dan e gloo
Fay mai whay.

Konz ploz be nat
Ontz non flatz woo
Rom katzem wolut Nantz a ku.

21. KATZEN, KATZEN

Katzen, Katzen in der Nacht
traeumen von der Seelachsschlacht!
Murrend, knurrend, zischend, jaulend
stemmen sie gegen je Morgengrauen.

Wo in Remscheid schwarze Daecher
aus Eifelschieferstein bestehen,

wenn auswaerts
Unschlitt
bestimmt
Kunstwelten,

wachen Katzen,
strecken sich sanft
zitternd
schaerfen Krallen und Zaehne
zu Hause knisternd.

Katzen, Katzen in der Nacht
traeumen von der Seelachsunschlittschlacht.

22. DEUTSCH IST EINE KATZENSPRACHE

Deutsch ist eine Katzensprache,
die zischt und knurrt und jault.
Wenn die Katze will, weil sie noch etwas wild ist,
knurrt sie und schleicht zwischen und um die Fuesse.

Wenn die Katze sich wehren will,
weil sie noch etwas wild ist,
zischt sie und reckt sich hoechst,
Krallen und Zaehne zeigend.

Wenn die Katze fressen will,
weil sie noch etwas wild ist,
jault sie laut in dem Wuestenhaus
bis sie Beute zerfleischt, knabbert und kaut.

Wenn die Katze froehlich ist,
weil sie noch etwas wild ist,
lauert sie still eine Zeit...
bis sie ploetzlich ausstoesst
und ueberaschend angreift.

23. WHEN YOU ARE THE CAPTAIN OF YOUR SHIP

1.

When you are the captain of your ship
you must know the shoals and read the rivulets
as they roll from the shores.
You must examine the sliding channels and check each
    roiling eddy.
Shallows must be shunned,
Plunging depths plumbed,
Accelerating currents exploited.

2.

When you are the captain of your ship
you must know what the whip in the wind and the
    sudden
sullen warm breeze and the still silence in between
mean
each one by one.
You must know why the air cools;
what to do if your jib is too stiff,
when to shut down and drop the sails.

You must know the winds like family
each one by name.

When Auster is angry
things that should not fly

fly.
Boreus will sometimes batter
even the best boat.
Sultry may Eurus be
and Zephyr hot and swift.
Confide in the winds when you feel it is right,
but be wary always.
They are as wild beasts.

3.

When you are the captain of your ship
you must know every eventuality of the sky,
the steady stars, the changing moons, the searing sun,
    the closely crowding clouds, the absolute blackness
    of night, the greys of the dawns and dusks and every
    which switch of light.

You must know when the waters mirror the heavens
    and
when they make mirages
of images and
tempting tones and
surreptitious shades;
when to trust what you see and
when to act on what you know
is not there.

4.

When you are the captain
you must know all personnel,
their needs, their talents, their weaknesses,

their strengths,
their debts…
their due;
when to settle all accounts
when to press an issue.

Learn to read their faces.
Learn how to parse their hearts.
Be loose when they need you to be.
Be tough when they need you to be.
You may need to be
more than you want to be.

5.

You must know your ship,
its every creak and groan
whenever it lurches and scrapes and
why
once the lines have gone too tentative and the hull has
    chided the reef
and you've underestimated the winds
and overestimated your crew
and she slowly winces
"Eeeeer! Eeeeeer! Eeeeeeeer!"
Then
after long deathly moments of excruciating silence
    the mast
SNAPS
and the sails tear
and your ship spins out of control.
You must know how to right it.
Calm it.

Stroke it.
Caress it.
Win it.
Make it trust you.
Make it love you as if it were
a beautiful seething wild woman.

6.

Finally
when you know all of this,
the water,
the wind,
the light,
your vessel,
all on board,
after you have righted your ship again and again
after sundry sudden storms;
shown your decisiveness to success,
your encouragement to rallies of support;
after you have keelhauled for insurgence,
given forgiveness whenever required and almost always
when requested,
after this
but only if
after all humiliations
good luck still is on your side
you may bring your ship with all on board
into safe harbor
to share your reward
and all and you
may rest then.

24. LIDIA

Was it a dream?

Was it a dream,
who drew my fancy
to cheerful eyes and thoughts that we
would dangle free
from fright and solitude?

Was it a dream,
who touched my lips with patient finger
and wrenched my heart with fever
to dance with glee
and freer
than the night shadowing our soul?

Was it a dream?

Was it a dream,
who said, "Yes!"
and
"Wait!'
and
"You have no idea how you please me!"
but
"Wait!"

and made no promises,
yet was all joy and sweet
and quiet mysteries of kisses and sleep?

25. THIS IS WHAT A REALLY GOOD POEM LOOKS LIKE/ THIS IS WHAT A REALLY GOOD POEM SOUNDS LIKE

For instructional purposes only

maggie and millie and molly and may (e.e. cummings)

maggie and millie and molly and may
went down to the beach (to play one day)

and maggie discovered a shell that sang
so sweetly she couldn't remember her troubles, and

millie befriended a stranded star
whose rays five languid fingers were;

and molly was chased by a horrible thing
which raced sideways while blowing bubbles; and

may came home with a smooth round stone
as small as a world and as large as alone.

For whatever we lose (like a you or a me)
it's always ourselves we find in the sea.

26. POEM ON THE SPIDEES
(unfinished)

Last night
when there were
no lights
the spinners came out like
countless times before
to thread their lines and weave their webs
to catch me.

Silent in their singular
sublime skillfulness
they went on their way
to make more means
to catch me,
them little spidees!

They sling their lines
time and again,
wait for firm attachment,
happy to sense
when their cobwebs go tense
so they'll not have to spin
another fine latch fence,
them little spidees!

27. RACCOON RENDEZVOUS or RING-TAIL ROMANCE

Midstride aside
elevated railroad lines
hardly detected metallic clicks
turn to metered snickers
and titters.
Ttttttll   ttttttll   d d d   ttttttll   ttttll
(like baseball cards clacking on bike spokes)
Manifold woolly silhouettes in the Eastern twilight
   theater
carve arched Kara Walker chiaroscuros.
Sinuous undulant shapes
on vertical planes unfurl and furl,
writhe thick and thin
on horizontal limbs
along filigree fingers
of oak and locust
lashed above the high horizon.
Rhomboid masks
freeze your gaze
on shadows deep
in the urban forest maze.
Fixed in surprise
by four eyes
made now motionless
there's barely time to assess,
if to fornicate
in a tree

happily
one truly needs complete privacy.

Startled looks like kids caught chocolate-smudged
raiding the cookie jar
won't hide their lusty earnest gambits
or hearty efforts to spawn new baby bandits.
There ain't no way to fudge
frolicsome raccoon love!
It's a frickin'
paw lickin'
furry fun fest!

28. NOW SMASH YOUR NASTY JAUNDICED JANUS FACE. THERE'S TIME TO SAVE YOUR SOUL

(a sonnet)

Now smash your nasty jaundiced Janus face
for it's unfair to judge you as you are.
You will not thrive at this lethargic pace.
Reclaim your balance; seek to find your star.

What once was fine exemplary behavior
has turned to foam-mouthed, wild-eyed vehemence
and stern self-righteous bashing of your neighbor.
Is your heart so feeble, so cold, your brain so dense?

Your handsome Janus face, the smiling one,
show to a world curious to see
a civil mensch bold in the golden sun.
Admit humbly your flawed humanity.

Courage, Faust, spurn Mephisto's hole!
Correct your course, there's time to save your soul.

29. MEMENTO MORI 2020

It was not so very long ago
we could play and laugh and grow.
Then oozed Grim Reaper from below
and took the life that we did know

and took the life that we did know.

Show devotion, stiff-armed salutes.
Don't think a moment he gives a hoot.
Ply Dear Leader with oleaginous praise.
He'll knife you in the back, give himself a raise.

When you see that bloated face
"Oy Gewalt" dear human race,
when you see that orange-hued clown,
flee fast away or all fall down.

It was not so very long ago,
there came a creature white eyes aglow
Don mano corto, the Mafioso
and took the life that we did know
and took the life that we did know.

Dance while you're able in your hallowed space.
Eat hearty and drink, if you find a place.
When one day came a dread disease
Masked Mephisto croaked, "It's a breeze!"

When you see that bloated face
"Oy Gewalt" dear human race,
when you see that white eyed clown
flee fast away or all fall down.

ABOUT THE AUTHOR

Steph Shearier lives in an aerie in Inwood, New York City with Maggie and Ulysses. Homer, Claire and Kleine are also there. For over 60 years he has carried on a shameless, open love affair with Mother Nature, while navigating homo sapien labyrinths in America and Deutschland. These poems, which deliberately incorporate old-school conventions, such as alliteration, onomatopoeia and internal rhyme, are crafted to conjure forgotten images. They may make you chuckle and might wrinkle your brow. With any luck they will underscore a rhythm in your head, you didn't know was there.

Best served while read aloud.